TOP MARKS

11 +

VERBAL REASONING

PRACTICE MAKES

PERFECT

40 QUESTIONS PER SECTION ON TOPICS COMMONLY TESTED IN THE 11+ EXAMINATION (WITH ANSWERS)

By Jane Stone

ISBN-13: 9781731083371

Acknowledgements

I would like to say a huge thank you to Dad and to my husband for helping me painstakingly check the questions and answers for any errors. It was quite a task. Hopefully, between us we have found any mistakes......apologies if not!

CONTENTS

Introduction

I have been a teacher for seventeen years and over the past ten years have tutored children in preparation for the 11 plus examination.

Over this time, I have frequently been asked by parents and students if there is a book they can purchase which provides multiple questions on topics which are causing difficulty and need to be practised. Sadly, to date, I have been unable to find one. So, I decided to write my own!

Many books are available to help teach the skills required to sit the 11 plus. Furthermore, there are many practice books on the market but none, that I have found, which offer more than a few questions on each topic.

Due to the requests I have received, I decided a book was needed which offered extensive work on many of the sections commonly tested in the 11 plus. My experience in Verbal Reasoning has been demonstrated by the marks my students consistently achieve in the tests, some have even attained full marks on this paper.

I hope my book will help your children to work on the areas they are finding challenging and as the adage states…….

….practice makes perfect.

Good luck with your studies!

1. Letter Sequences

A B C D E F G H I J K L M N O P Q R S T U V W X Y Z

Example: AK   BH   CE   DB.......   Answer: EY

1st letter - move forward in the alphabet 1 letter each time: A B C D....**E**

2nd letter – move backwards in the alphabet 3 letters each time: K H E B....**Y**

Multiple Choice Answers

1.   BX EV HT KR -----   MP NR NP OR OQ

2.   MN HR CV XZ -----   PQ SD RM SE PR

3.   OQ MS KU IW -----   GY FY GW FX GX

4.   EU GT JR NO -----   PK RL RK SK SL

5.   BY DW FU HS -----   JQ IT IQ JU JW

6.   JK LM OO SQ -----   UR VS VT XS XT

7.   EB EZ FX FV -----   GV GX FT GT FV

8.   PQ OR NS MT -----   QT RT QU LU LV

9.   HE KB NY QV -----   RS ST TS TT SW

10. UA TZ SY RX -----   WQ WT QW QV QX

11. RE PI NM LQ -----   IJ JU KU IV IT

12. AZ CX EV GT -----　　　HR HI IR IS JS

13. HW IV KT NQ -----　　　PM PN QN RN RM

14. OP OU MS MX -----　　　JT KP JV KV OV

15. ZT BS DQ FN -----　　　IJ IK HJ HK JJ

16. NT PQ RN TK -----　　　WH VH WG VG WI

17. BP ZT XX VB -----　　　UC TD TF UF UB

18. HK MM RO WQ -----　　　AS BS CS BR CR

19. EM DN CO BP -----　　　BQ DQ AQ AR BR

20. GR IP KN ML -----　　　NO NJ ON OJ OL

21. ON PM RK UH -----　　　YD XD YE XE YC

22. VE XB ZY BV -----　　　ES DS ET BT DT

23. JF OG SI VL -----　　　YO XP YP XO ZP

24. CT CV EX EZ -----　　　EA EB GA GB FB

25. NM PN NO PP -----　　　PQ NR NQ PP NP

26. WA VC TE QG -----　　　MJ NH NI LJ MI

27. SH OK KN GQ -----　　　CT DU BU DT CS

28. YT ZU AV BW -----　　　DZ DX CX DY CY

29. HA FA DB BB -----   AC ZB YA YB ZC

30. LZ FB ZD TF -----   OD NI MH NH MI

31. BR FN JJ NF -----   RA SC RB QA SB

32. MR OP QN SL -----   VI UJ VJ WH UI

33. SH VJ YL BN -----   DQ EP DO DP EO

34. JO KN ML PI -----   SE SD TD TE UD

35. KA MC IE KG -----   MH GH MD GJ GI

36. DS CR FU ET -----   GV FW HW FX HV

37. RB OF LJ IN -----   ES FR GR GS FT

38. MP JQ HR ES -----   BS BU CS BT CT

39. HI GJ FK EL -----   DL CM DN DM CN

40. ZY CV FS IP -----   JN KM LN KN LM

2. Letter Pairs

A B C D E F G H I J K L M N O P Q R S T U V W X Y Z

Example: GM is to JL as RV is to......   Answer: UU

The first letter in the first pair, G, moves forward 3 letters to get to the first letter in the second pair, J. So move forward 3 letters from R, the first letter in the second pair to get U.

The second letter in the first pair, M, moves back 1 letter to get to the second letter in the second pair, L. So move back 1 letter from V, the second letter in the second pair to get U.

Multiple Choice Answers

1. FJ is to BM as PT is to -----   TQ TW LW LV MW

2. BY is to DW as CX is to -----   DU EV AU EW AV

3. GM is to LI as OJ is to -----   TD SF TE TF UE

4. RA is to OE as BH is to -----   YM ZK ZM YK YL

5. SZ is to RA as AY is to -----   ZZ ZA YY BZ BY

6. NN is to GR as PC is to -----   JH IG JF IF JG

7. PQ is to MT as VT is to -----   RX SW SV QX RW

8. ER is to AT as FD is to -----   AF BE BG BF CF

9. FQ is to KS as BH is to -----   FJ GI GJ GK FI

10. WV is to AS as YM is to -----   CK EI DJ CJ DI

11. OO is to PN as TT is to -----   UT UV US SS ST

12. HG is to EM as KN is to -----   HT HS GT HU GS

13. AZ is to BY as CX is to -----   BV DV BX BW DW

14. CI is to VN as HU is to -----   AP AZ AA OP OZ

15. DM is to GP as SF is to -----   VK UI VI WH VJ

16. IT is to FR as TN is to -----   QL QK RL QM RJ

17. JJ is to HM as QQ is to -----   SU OU OS SS OT

18. KR is to LL as DH is to -----   CB EB CC EC EA

19. LW is to HX as AB is to -----   EC WA DC WC EA

20. MC is to JI as SW is to -----   PC OC PB OA QC

21. NP is to PN as RR is to -----   PP TT TP PO PT

22. QL is to UK as CT is to -----   FU GV FS GU GS

23. TO is to QR as JD is to -----   MA MG MH GG GF

24. UB is to AX as IV is to -----   OQ OR OS CR DS

25. VS is to PY as NF is to -----   GK GL HM HL GM

26. XD is to SH as LR is to -----   GV HU GW FW FV

27. YM is to CK as OH is to -----   SE RJ SJ RF SF

28. ZJ is to TO as PB is to -----   JF VF JG JE VG

29. AL is to FK as KT is to -----   OS QR PR OR PS

30. BR is to UN as FL is to -----   YI YH YP XH XP

31. CR is to GV as MO is to -----   QS RS QR QT PS

32. FN is to CT as VX is to -----   SE YC SD YD SC

33. LA is to MZ as DR is to -----   EQ CP EP CS DQ

34. WI is to PK as NP is to -----   UQ GR GS UR TR

35. JP is to FT as BC is to -----   XF FE XG XH FG

36. DT is to KO as LI is to -----   SD SE EN SN EF

37. IU is to JT as EL is to -----   EN FK FJ FL EK

38. WL is to ZJ as YU is to -----   BS ZS AR BT BR

39. OG is to TD as GS is to -----   LR LQ MQ LP KP

40. RH is to MJ as WT is to -----   SW RV QX QV RX

3. Three Letter Words

Example: I HED my homework in on time.

(RAN, AND, END, ICE, ACE)

Select a three-letter word, from the multiple-choice answers, which will complete the partial word in capitals. Think of a word which makes the sentence make sense. The three-letter word can be inserted anywhere in the word but must stay in order and you must not rearrange any of the other letters.

Answer: AND   I h**and**ed my homework in on time.

Multiple Choice Answers in brackets

1. Where can I ST my belongings?
   (ALL, END, ORE, ASK, ARE)

2. Paul tried to PRED he had not heard his mum calling!
   (TON, TAN, TEN, SIT, SAT)

3. The storm HAPED during the night.
   (PAN, DEN, PEN, PIN, PUN)

4. Claire SNED the room searching for her friend.
   (CAR, TAN, PEN, CAN, CAT)

5. The CN at the circus made everybody laugh.
   (LIE, APE, ART, LOW, LAP)

6. The picnic HER was filled with delicious food.
   (IMP, EAT TEA, FOR, AMP)

7. A large EXSION was built on the back of the house.
   (TEN, MEN, MAN, TON, PEN)

8. Chopping the ONS made my eyes water!
   (ARE, ION, TAR, HOT, TAP)

9. The policeman thought the story was FABRIED.
   (SAT, MAT, DIE, CAT, DAY)

10. The recipe was easy providing you FOLED the instructions.
    (LAW, ICE, LOW, ACE, BAN)

11. A brightly coloured FHER decorated the girl's hat.
(ACE, ICE, EAT, ATE, TEA)

12. The child carefully TRD the picture.
(PAR, APE, ACE, ART, ICE)

13. It was the NST eclair she had ever tasted.
(ACE, HOP, LAP, END, ICE)

14. The flowers in the vase HERED without water.
(TAP, WIT, SIT, WET, WAS)

15. As the marathon entered the final mile many runners became TD.
(OLD, ORE, IRE, ARE, RAN)

16. The tree's BCHES waved in the wind.
(AND, RAN, LOW, RAW, LAW)

17. I love SES with jam and cream.
(COW, CAN, CON, TAN, TON)

18. The walker packed a FL of tea to take on his hike.
(AND, ASK, ART, END, EGG)

19. When it was fully GN my sunflower was over a metre tall!
(ROW, RAW, RAN, SOW, SAW)

20. We live in a beautiful TCHED cottage in the countryside,
(HIT, HOT, HAT, RAP, RAT)

21. I always do my supermarket SPING on Friday.
(HOP, HIP, RIP, LOW, ROB)

22. After a long day at work Mrs. Jones felt very WY.
(EAR, EYE, TOE, AGE, ANT)

23. Tom spent the ST amount of time possible on his homework!
(MOP, LEA, BEE, SAT, GET)

24. The TRUM is my favourite instrument in the brass section.
(PIT, POT, PUT, PET, PAT)

25. My brother BGED about winning the football tournament.
(RUG, RAG, RIG, LAG, END)

26. In the sale lots of prices were UCED.
   (RED, RID, ROD, DIG, TRY)

27. The door HLE was covered in sticky fingerprints.
   (END, AND, SAW, DUG, BAG)

28. Our roof has SL tiles.
   (ART, ANT, ICE, ACE, ATE)

29. The vase SMED into hundreds of tiny pieces.
   (PIN, PUT, HAT, ASH, AND)

30. The painting was HID under an old blanket.
   (SAG, RED, BET, DEN, BEG)

31. The chief of the TE is a very powerful person.
   (ROB, RIB, RUB, RAT, RIG)

32. Yesterday, I bought a new pair of SS.
   (HAT, BAG, HOE, HOT, LOT)

33. MR. Brown was delighted to be promoted to AGER.
   (MEN, MAN, MET, TUG, TOE)

34. The WEAR is very unpredictable, even in the summer.
   (TEN, TEE, TON, THE, TEA)

35. The learner driver turned the steering WH very cautiously.
   (ALE, AIL, EEL, ATE, OLD)

36. I always SD too much when I go shopping.
   (TEN, TAN, PEN, PAN, PUT)

37. The Christmas stocking was EN with gifts.
   (BIG, LID, LAD, CUT, BUT)

38. Water was in SCE supply during the drought.
   (HOT, ARC, ACE, CAN, LOW)

39. I keep my precious TRETS in a special box.
   (INK, EAR, ICE, BAN, BIT)

40. The millionaire lived in an enormous SION.
   (TAN, MEN, MAN, PAN, PEN)

4. Odd Words Out

Example: taste, sweet, touch, smell, odour

Select two words from the list which do not belong in the same group as the other three.

Answer: sweet, odour
The other words are all senses. Sweet and odour are not.

Select and underline two words from each list.

1. shade, sun, hue, hot, colour

2. grin, dash, race, discover, sprint

3. saunter, fly, swim, sidle, amble

4. sail, swim, relay, canoe, hurdle

5. tennis, football, badminton, rugby, squash

6. gold, silver, ruby, emerald, sapphire

7. club, spade, foot, liver, heart

8. fur, lace, scales, plastic, feathers

9. pint, gallon, litre, gram, metre

10. cabbage, apple, carrot, potato, pear

11. cotton, iron, steel, denim, gold

12. train, paddock, field, bicycle, scooter

13. touch, taste, view, cold, sight

14. prime, paint, add, odd, even

15. author, composer, book, poet, music

16. mug, cup, fork, assault, attack

17. hamper, aid, assist, hinder, help

18. fork, knife, plate, spade, spoon

19. bag, basket, cap, shoe, holdall

20. call, look, brooch, watch, ring

21. river, sky, air, stream, brook

22. torch, lantern, table, phone, candle

23. sketch, draw, latch, doodle, point

24. jack, jester, lady, king, ace

25. raven, knight, queen, battle, rook

26. finger, card, chapter, index, glossary

27. letter, colon, apostrophe, sentence, hyphen

28. second, third, minute, tiny, hour

29. day, minute, small, tomorrow, petite

30. iris, daisy, pupil, school, retina

31. swallow, gulp, dodge, duck, sparrow

32. wise, wisdom, molar, cut, incisor

33. stamp, bang, letter, envelope, word

34. film, play, record, concert, radio

35. stem, support, leaf, start, root

36. kiwi, red, onion, lemon, mango

37. cherry, sea, ruby, sky, blood

38. wasp, bee, worm, ladybird, snail

39. cheese, mouse, piano, keyboard, monitor

40. mare, stallion, ewe, bull, boar

5. Moving A Letter

Example: plate clam

Remove one letter from the first word, it can be any of the letters, to make a new word.

Move the letter into the second word to make another new word. Again, the letter can be placed anywhere in the second word.

Answer: p   new words: late and clamp

Select one letter from the first word		Answer
1. stand	race	S T A N D
2. droop	pen	D R O O P
3. shied	con	S H I E D
4. steep	breath	S T E E P
5. noise	most	N O I S E
6. horse	gain	H O R S E
7. cloud	lay	C L O U D
8. spite	lane	S P I T E
9. batch	sold	B A T C H
10. stung	plea	S T U N G
11. cloth	same	C L O T H
12. gripe	vent	G R I P E
13. proud	clod	P R O U D
14. plain	sad	P L A I N
15. flake	four	F L A K E
16. feast	tones	F E A S T
17. ounce	pond	O U N C E

18. scale	reed	S C A L E
19. flown	live	F L O W N
20. haven	eater	H A V E N
21. pinch	late	P I N C H
22. saved	ream	S A V E D
23. float	hard	F L O A T
24. wider	gate	W I D E R
25. pride	sore	P R I D E
26. wager	gaze	W A G E R
27. snake	sore	S N A K E
28. store	lime	S T O R E
29. tease	spoil	T E A S E
30. dread	boar	D R E A D
31. waver	bead	W A V E R
32. brake	con	B R A K E
33. choke	ail	C H O K E
34. farce	cove	F A R C E
35. ghost	stun	G H O S T
36. patch	laws	P A T C H
37. pitch	lamp	P I T C H
38. bland	drive	B L A N D
39. wrist	wait	W R I S T
40. whine	sows	W H I N E

6. Start/End Letters

Example: tai ( ) ance   ful ( ) ever

Multiple choice answers: d n l p e

Find a letter which ends the first word and starts the second word. The letter must be correct for all four words.

Answer: l   **words are tail, lance, full and lever**

			Multiple Choice Answers
1. ben ( ) ark	lan ( ) upe		t e d p l
2. pat ( ) and	pit ( ) old		b c h l f
3. dra ( ) ind	flo ( ) ear		g m e t w
4. buo ( ) arn	tra ( ) ield		m y d s f
5. are ( ) lly	quot ( ) rid		o, e, t ,a, i
6. car ( ) pic	min ( ) dge		t, e, s, o, d
7. gru ( ) all	cri ( ) ind		w, f, r, b, t
8. puf ( ) ort	cuf ( ) lan		e, t, f, s, b
9. dra ( ) ong	lon ( ) nat		b, r, e, g, w
10. fee ( ) ace	spoi ( ) imp		d, t, l, f, r
11. fil ( ) ace	har ( ) etre		l, m, e, p, f

12. com ( ) land	thum ( ) row	e, p, g, s, b
13. fea ( ) ich	lia ( ) uby	t, d, m, r, y
14. plu ( ) ting	glas ( ) lay	g, s, p, t, w
15. cas ( ) are	wis ( ) ind	t, r, e, f, h
16. was ( ) ilt	clas ( ) erd	t, p, h, w, e
17. dru ( ) lare	sin ( ) lint	t, m, e, g, f
18. win ( ) erm	fla ( ) entle	p, m, t, e, g
19. wic ( ) ing	luc ( ) eel	f, r, h, k, m
20. sig ( ) ail	fla ( ) eat	h, n, s, p, r
21. ceas ( ) arn	tir ( ) asy	s, y, e, p, t
22. wra ( ) our	cla ( ) rance	w, f, p, s, t
23. glo ( ) and	ste ( ) hat	s, t, w, b, c
24. so ( ) here	cro ( ) ilt	b, r, e, t, w
25. fi ( ) aint	gloa ( ) oil	t, g, b, p, s
26. fli ( ) rim	hin ( ) ale	p, g, t, s, m
27. grat ( ) arn	rov ( ) ase	y, b, d, l, e
28. blu ( ) eap	sca ( ) aw	s, b, p, r, t

29. clu ( ) ran	or ( ) unch	c, l, k, b, g
30. sas ( ) ail	clot ( ) andle	p, y, j, h, n
31. tic ( ) erb	trac ( ) ilt	h, e, b, k, d
32. ha ( ) acht	angr ( ) ear	t, f, y, d, w
33. hal ( ) nly	her ( ) ily	e, l, t, o, p
34. fee ( ) oud	crue ( ) ead	t, r, d, m, l
35. er ( ) ngle	are ( ) rmy	n, l, i, e, a
36. hym ( ) ot	pi ( ) et	m, p, t, n, l
37. san ( ) esk	clou ( ) are	g, e, d, t, w
38. far ( ) int	gri ( ) are	m, e, p, s, l
39. sli ( ) roud	har ( ) ant	t, k, d, p, e
40. acto ( ) ace	bea ( ) ear	n, m, p, r, l

7. Words With Two Meanings

Example: (hut, tent)   shack, shelter, camp, home, defend
(protect, shield)

Select the answer which will go equally well with both pairs of words.
Answer: shelter
A hut/tent is a kind of shelter and if you protect/shield something you shelter it.

Multiple Choice Answers

1. (business, company)
(hard, solid)   rigid, organisation, firm, rock, corporation

2. (sugary, confectionary)
(kind, lovely)   pudding, considerate, dessert, sweet

3. (construct, make)
(boat, barge)   yacht, dinghy, model, craft, design

4. (dismiss, sack)
(blaze, inferno)   flame, remove, fire, discard, candle

5. (pester, annoy)
(epidemic, disease)   irritate, illness, virus, plague, cold

6. (challenge, overcome)
(equipment, gear)   tools, tackle, face, implements, beat

7. (break, fracture)
(photograph, picture)   painting, sketch, snap, shatter, crack

8. (furniture, seat)
(leader, supervisor)   sofa, boss, head, chair, settee

9. (record, note)
(timber, wood)   journal, diary, log, tree, branch

10. (irate, angry)
(bisect, intersect)   cut, cross, livid, annoy, divide

11. (sparkle, glow)
(polish, buff)

shine, bright, glare, clean, dust

12. (marina, quay)
(shelter, shield)

cover, cushion, mooring, harbour, berth

13. (gale, hurricane)
(barge, charge)

tornado, wind, crash, storm, fight

14. (pull, tug)
(catch, amount)

quantity, number, haul, halt, drag

15. (jacket, anorak)
(cover, layer)

fleece, coat, blanket, duvet, blazer

16. (rain, drizzle)
(spoil, lavish)

downpour, extravagant, shower, storm, treat

17. (thwart, defeat)
(material, metal)

beat, overcome, element, foil, substance

18. (material, covering)
(touched, handled)

stroke, felt, cloth, cotton, sheet

19. (engine, locomotive)
(teach instruct)

tutor, car, machine, guide, train

20. (stop, quell)
(stalk, plant)

leaf, petal, cease, stem, quit

21. (light, blonde)
(just, appropriate)

bleached, apt, golden, right, fair

22. (stick, support)
(hit, beat)

smack, thump, cane, post, bump

23. (pudding, dessert)
(unimportant, insignificant)

sweet, trivial, petty, trifle, confectionary

24. (reptile, viper)
(twist, turn)

rotate, spin, snake, asp, lizard

25. (season, spice)
(sprinkle, add)

flavour, scatter, pepper, taste, throw

26. (move, alter)
(rota, work)

budge, change, turn, schedule, shift

27. (drink, juice)
(press, squeeze)

flatten, squash, cordial, liquid, iron

28. (holiday, excursion)
(fall, stumble)

break, vacation, tumble, trip, overbalance

29. (number, digit)
(statue, sculpture)

bronze, figure, carving, finger, value

30. (crossword, logic)
(think, ponder)

consider, decide, sudoku, jigsaw, puzzle

31. (press, flatten)
(metal, element)

squash, smooth, material, hard, iron

32. (dish, container)
(deliver, throw)

post, tureen, send, bowl, box

33. (mirror, image)
(think, consider)

ponder, deliberate, reflect, shine, copy

34. (hit, strike)
(strap, band)

thump, club, tie, belt, leash

35. (copy, reflect)
(looking-glass, surface)

shine, image, replicate, mirror, ape

36. (search, look)
(tool, implement)

seek, scan, comb, brush, scour

37. (protect, shield)
(darkness, cover)

cushion, block, shelter, dim, shade

38. (animal, canine)
(pursue, follow)

pet, mammal, track, dog, trail

39. (tear, tug)
(tool, implement)

heave, spanner, saw, wrench, pull

40. (succeed, success)
(move, throw)

win, triumph, lob, pass, hurl

8. Hidden Four Letter Words

Example: A sudden tremor violently shook the building.

Find a four-letter word hidden between two of the words in the sentence.

Answer: dent

A sud<u>den t</u>remor violently shook the building.

1. The girl delivered each invitation personally.

2. Follow the path into the woods.

3. Which operation will solve the problem?

4. We really love our new car.

5. The match seemed to be over.

6. Pay the same attention when crossing the street.

7. The teacher gave me extra maths homework.

8. "Are you awake?" she called gently.

9. "This is amazing!" she said eagerly

10. It is our favourite time of year.

11. We listened to the instructions carefully.

12. Always eat fruit and vegetables every day.

13. The city really buzzed with excitement.

14. Ensure you pay your tax immediately.

15. Each entrance was very clearly signposted.

16. His inkling was to turn right.

17. This story is full of mystery.

18. We agreed that everybody should have a vote.

19. The girl sang like a little angel.

20. Please attach the form to your letter.

21. The sign attached to the gate said, beware.

22. Children need safe areas in which to play.

23. The bus fare always increases annually.

24. Be careful not to harm yourself.

25. The woman told the doctor about her ailments.

26. Book your annual leave in October.

27. Please empty the bins every day.

28. I hope nobody forgets their homework.

29. Simon was too lazy to tidy his bedroom.

30. I love nibbling chocolate biscuits with my coffee.

31. The fox entered the chicken house after dark.

32. Our flight to Spain was in the morning.

33. We had to label two diagrams in Science.

34. My sister did her best to win the competition.

35. The robot's eyes flashed red then blue.

36. Stick extra tape around the parcel.

37. We must pay our bills on time.

38. Jo tried to grab all the sweets.

39. His oily overalls needed a long soak.

40. The alarm went off after midnight.

9. Solving Algebra Equations

Example: If   A= 8   B=5   C=10   D=6   E=2

Find: D (C / E)

Answer: 10/ 2 = 5 x 6 = 30   (when there is no sign multiply ie D x (C/E)

Sometimes the answer is given as a **letter** so one the numbers in the question will be the answer.

Example: AE – D   (AE means A x E)

Answer: 8 x 2 = 16 – 6 = 10

As C = 10 the letter C is the answer.

For the following questions give your answer as a number.

Question 1

If   A = 1   B = 2   C = 5   D = 8   E = 10

Solve the following:	**Multiple Choice Answers**
i. D (E / C)	14, 15, 16, 17, 18
ii. D + B – A	11, 10, 9, 8, 7
iii. CD – B	40, 38, 36, 34, 32
iv. C (D / B) – A	15, 17, 19, 21, 23
v. BCE	40, 70, 80, 100, 160

Question 2

If   A = 4   B = 7   C = 9   D = 11   E = 20

Solve the following: **Multiple Choice Answers**

   i.   CD – B   90, 81, 92, 56, 103

   ii.   A + B – D   2, 0, 20, 6, 27

   iii. B (E / A) + C   45, 44, 43, 42, 41

   iv. E – D – B   0, 2, 4, 6, 8

   v.   AD + E   60, 64, 81, 69, 84

Question 3

If   A = 6   B = 8   C = 12   D = 15   E = 30

Solve the following: **Multiple Choice Answers**

   i.   B (E / A)   20, 40, 60, 80, 100

   ii.   AB + C   60, 78, 63, 65, 70

   iii. A (C / B) + E   34, 35, 37, 39, 40

   iv. D + C + A – B   20, 25, 30, 35, 40

   v.   BC + D – A   95 100 105 110 115

Question 4

If A = 3   B = 7   C = 11   D = 9   E = 2

Solve the following: **Multiple Choice Answers**

   i.   AB + C – E   28, 30, 32, 34, 36

  ii.   CD + B – A   97, 100, 103, 106, 109

 iii.   C (D / A) + B   42, 40, 38, 36, 34

 iv.   E + B + C + D   27, 28, 29, 30, 31

  v.   B + A + C – E   15, 16, 17, 18, 19

For the following questions give your answer as a letter.

Question 5

If A = 2   B = 6   C = 4   D = 10   E = 20

Solve the following: **Multiple Choice Answers**

   i.   A (E / D)   A   B   C   D   E

  ii.   D – B – A   A   B   C   D   E

 iii.   A (E / C)   A   B   C   D   E

 iv.   D + B + C   A   B   C   D   E

  v.   E / A – C   A   B   C   D   E

Question 6

If A = 4   B = 3   C = 15   D = 1   E = 20

Solve the following: **Multiple Choice Answers**

  i.   B (E / A)   A B C D E

  ii.   E − C − A   A B C D E

  iii. A (C / B)   A B C D E

  iv. AB + B   A B C D E

  v.   C / D / B − D   A B C D E

Question 7

If A = 9   B = 1   C = 2   D = 12   E = 25

Solve the following: **Multiple Choice Answers**

  i.   CD + B   A B C D E

  ii.   D / C + B + C   A B C D E

  iii. A + C + B   A B C D E

  iv. E + A − D − A − B   A B C D E

  v.   D − A − B   A B C D E

Question 8

If A = 8   B = 14   C = 7   D = 3   E = 10

Solve the following;   **Multiple Choice Answers**

  i.   CD – B   A B C D E

  ii.   AD – B   A B C D E

  iii. A + C + D – E   A B C D E

  iv. B – E + D   A B C D E

  v.   E (B / C) – E – C   A B C D E

10. Completing A Number Sentence

Example: 6 x 3 + 2 = 24 - ?

Calculate: 6 x 3 + 2 = 20

So 24 - ? = 20

? = 4

Replace the ? with a number

Multiple Choice Answers

1. 3 x 4 + 6 = 27 - ?   8   9   10   12   18

2. 20 / 4 x 6 = 60 / ?   2   4   6   8   10

3. 19 + 7 – 4 = 18 + ?   4   8   12   22   24

4. 30 + 5 – 2 = 6 x ? + 9   2   3   4   5   6

5. 40 / 8 x 7 + 5 = ? – 20   40   50   60   70   80

6. 3 x 3 x 3 + 4 = 3 x ? + 10   3   7   10   12   15

7. 32 / 4 x 2 + 8 = ? – 6   28   30   32   34   36

8. (12 + 15) / 3 = 2 x 4 + ?   0   1   2   3   4

9. 81 / 9 x 2 +10 = ? / 2 +18   14   16   18   20   22

10. (7 x 6) / 2 + 9 = 6 x ? + 12   2   3   4   5   6

11. 15 + 7 + 11 = 11 x ?   1   2   3   4   5

12.42 + 16 − 12 = 12 x ? − 2   2 3 4 5 6

13.2 x 3 x 4 + 12 = 5 x ? + 1   2 3 5 7 10

14.50 − 7 − 5 − 3 = 6 x ? + 5   1 3 5 7 9

15.(10 − 4) + 7 = 2 x ? + 3 =   1 2 3 4 5

16.7 x 8 − 2 = 100 / 2 + ?   2 4 8 12 20

17.11 x 7 + 4 = 9 x ?   6 7 8 9 10

18.20 x 4 − 6 = 10 x ? + 4   6 7 9 11 15

19.144 / 12 x 8 = 24 x 2 x ?   2 3 4 5 6

20.(100 − 12) + 2 = ? x 8 − 6   4 8 12 16 20

21.16 + 9 = 5 x ?   3 4 5 6 7

22.24 + 6 − 2 = 7 x ?   3 4 5 6 7

23.62 + 8 − 1 = 8 x ? + 5   6 8 10 12 14

24.72 / 8 x 3 = 2 x ? + 7   0 5 10 15 20

25.54 / 9 x 5 = 17 + ?   11 12 13 14 15

26.63 / 7 x 4 = ? + 6   26 30 32 36 40

27.74 − 7 = ? x 6 + 1   11 13 15 17 19

28. $68 - 5 = 9 \times \, ?$ 4 5 6 7 8

29. $96 / 8 \times 4 = \, ? \times 4 + 8$ 8 9 10 11 12

30. $16 / 2 \times 3 + 6 = \, ? \times 2 + 6$ 9 10 11 12 13

31. $11 \times 6 + 3 = \, ? \times 3 + 9$ 10 15 20 25 30

32. $80 - 7 - 3 = 6 \times \, ? - 2$ 11 12 13 14 15

33. $15 \times 2 + 10 = \, ? + 14$ 20 26 28 32 36

34. $30 \times 3 - 7 = \, ? \times 2 + 3$ 32 36 40 44 50

35. $70 / 2 - 3 = 2 \times 8 \times \, ?$ 1 2 3 4 5

36. $56 / 7 + 4 - 6 = 9 \times 2 - \, ?$ 4 8 12 16 20

37. $4 \times 7 + 11 + 4 = 6 \times 8 - \, ?$ 3 5 7 9 11

38. $144 / 12 + 5 - 2 = 20 / \, ? \times 3$ 1 2 4 5 10

39. $6 \times 5 \times 2 - 3 = 30 + \, ? + 19$ 5 7 8 10 12

40. $8 \times 6 + 6 - 2 = \, ? \times 2 + 2$ 9 16 25 36 49

11. Completing A Number Sequence

Example: 3, 5, 8, 12, 17, ?

Find the pattern and continue the sequence.

Answer: $3 + 2 = 5 + 3 = 8 + 4 = 12 + 5 = 17 + 6 = 23$

The pattern is add 2 add 3 add 4 add 5 so continue by adding 6 to 17

Answer: 23

Sometimes there are two patterns

Example: 2, 5, 4, 10, 6, 15, 8, ?

First pattern: +2 $2 + 2 = 4 + 2 = 6 + 2 = 8$

Second pattern:+5 $5 + 5 = 10 + 5 = 15 + 5 = 20$

Answer: 20

Multiple Choice Answers

1. 6, 7, 8, 9, 11, 11,	?	12 14 15 16 18
2. 2, 4, 8, 16, 32,	?	40 54 60 64 70
3. 12, 15, 14, 17, 16, 19,	?	16 17 18 19 20
4. 64, 59, 54, 49, 44,	?	33 35 37 39 41
5. 1, 1, 2, 6, 24,	?	48 60 100 120 140
6. 30, 27, 35, 30, 40, 33	?	35 40 45 50 55

7. 72, 76, 74, 78, 76,   ?   78 80 82 84 86

8. 84, 74, 65, 57, 50,   ?   41 42 43 44 45

9. 101, 91, 82, 74, 67,   ?   59 60 61 62 63

10.2, 2, 4, 12, 48,   ?   96 144 192 240 288

11.90, 87, 95, 83, 100, 79, 105,   ?   75 85 95 105 115

12.180, 90, 92, 46, 48,   ?   20 24 36 38 50

13.57, 63, 61, 67, 65,   ?   70 71 72 73 74

14.89,90,86,88,84,87,   ?   83 84 85 86 88

15.76, 71, 74, 69, 73, 68   ?   63 65 67 70 73

16.100, 99, 96, 105, 92, 111,   ?   78 88 98 108 118

17.23, 29, 25, 28, 27, 27, 29,   ?   24 26 27 29 31

18.4, 24, 8, 12, 12, 6, 16,   ?   2 3 8 14 20

19.87, 31, 77, 41, 67, 51,   ?   54 55 56 57 58

20.72, 54, 36, 57, 12, 60,   ?   3 9 12 43 63

21.100, 60, 50, 80, 25, 100,   ?   6.5 12.5 20.5 75 120

22.42, 58, 49, 60, 56, 62,   ?   60 61 62 63 64

23.64, 49, 36, 25, 16,   ?   4 6 9 12 15

24.73, 75, 71, 73, 69,	?	67 68 70 71 73
25.85, 86, 88, 91, 95,	?	97 98 99 100 101
26.8, 4, 12, 16, 28,	?	34 38 42 44 48
27.90, 45, 46, 23, 24,	?	18 16 12 10 8
28.37, 26, 47, 29, 57,	?	28 32 45 50 67
29.5, 3, 8, 11, 19,	?	26 28 30 32 34
30.40, 30, 20, 60, 10, 120,	?	5 10 20 50 100
31.1, 3, 6, 10, 15,	?	20 21 22 23 24
32.3, 3, 6, 18, 72,	?	216 288 360 400 420
33.5, 7, 10, 14, 19,	?	25 26 27 28 29
34.1, 5, 20, 60, 120,	?	15 30 60 120 240
35.47, 46, 44, 41, 37,	?	29 30 31 32 33
36.33, 35, 34, 36, 35,	?	36 37 38 39 40
37.26, 36, 25, 35, 26,	?	30 34 36 45 55
38.54, 47, 41, 36, 32,	?	27 28 29 30 31
39.7, 9, 13, 21. 37,	?	58 63 66 69 72
40.200, 120, 80, 60, 50,	?	25 30 35 40 45

12. Find The Missing Middle Number

Example: 2 (8) 32 　　　3 (12) 48 　　　　4 ( ) 64

Multiply each number by 4. 　　2 x 4 = 8 x 4 = 32
　　　　　　　　　　　　　　　3 x 4 = 12 x 4 = 48
　　　　　　　　　　　　　　　4 x 4 = 16 x 4 = 64

Answer: 16

			Multiple Choice Answers
1. 3 (9) 27	4 (8) 16	5 (　) 80	10 15 20 25 30
2. 24 (19) 14	37 (32) 27	46 (　) 36	37 38 39 41 43
3. 50 (44) 38	34 (26) 18	41 (　) 31	35 36 37 38 39
4. 48 (39) 9	62 (54) 8	32 (　) 7	21 22 23 24 25
5. 12 (9) 6	14 (10) 6	18 (　) 6	10 12 14 16 18
6. 40 (20) 10	60 (30) 15	80 (　) 20	30 35 40 45 50
7. 6 (30) 9	8 (44) 14	7 (　) 7	14 16 20 28 494
8. 6 (10) 15	12 (15) 19	18 (　) 33	21 22 23 24 25
9. 24 (21) 19	38 (34) 31	47 (　) 28	30 33 37 39 43
10. 7 (14) 42	3 (6) 18	4 (　) 24	5 6 7 8 9

11. 5 (7) 9   8 (9) 10   12 (   ) 8   7 8 9 10 11

12. 24 (30) 36   19 (25) 31   35 (   ) 47   37 39 41 43 45

13. 2(6) 12   5 (15) 30   8 (   ) 48   16 24 32 40 44

14. 48 (12) 4   24 (6) 2   12 (   ) 1   1 2 3 4 6

15. 32 (27) 22   46 (41) 36   57 (   ) 47   50 51 52 53 54

16. 6 (20) 10   8 (26) 14   12 (   ) 15   30 31 32 33 34

17. 100 (75) 50   75 (52) 32   90 (   ) 30   50 55 60 65 70

18. 1 (5) 25   3 (9) 27   2 (   ) 72   8 10 12 14 16

19. 21 (28) 36   42 (49) 57   53 (   ) 68   52 55 57 60 61

20. 8 (60) 12   7 (36) 5   9 (   ) 6   15 30 45 60 75

21. 2 (20) 200   6 (60) 600   12 (   ) 1200   120 140 160 180 200

22. 24 (18) 13   18 (26) 35   27 (   ) 42   32 34 36 38 40

23. 2 (4) 16   3 (6) 24   10 (   ) 80   12 15 20 22 25

24. 16 (30) 14   21 (46) 25   36 (   ) 38   71 72 73 74 75

25. 56 (32) 24   61 (32) 29   78 (   ) 34   14 24 34 44 54

26. 62 (58) 55   78 (73) 69   56 (   ) 55   51 52 53 54 55

27. 42 (11) 20   54 (15) 24   68 (   ) 32   10 14 18 22 26

28. 14 (20) 9   16 (16) 12   20 (   ) 12   20 26 30 32 40

29. 6 (10) 14   9 (11) 13   15 (   ) 27   17 19 21 23 25

30. 18 (10) 2   21 (12) 3   35 (   ) 3   15 19 21 24 30

31. 76 (73) 70   46 (42) 38   96 (   ) 82   89 90 91 92 93

32. 7 (19) 5   3 (10) 4   10 (   ) 7   17 22 24 27 30

33. 43 (8) 35   36 (5) 31   52 (   ) 46   2 3 4 5 6

34. 70 (7) 10   50 (10) 5   40 (   ) 2   5 8 10 20 40

35. 19 (22) 26   37 (40) 44   56 (   ) 63   57 58 59 60 61

36. 6 (24) 4   7 (21) 3   8 (   ) 9   54 63 72 81 90

37. 21 (28) 35   46 (42) 38   32 (   ) 42   35 36 37 38 3.9

38. 21 (7) 3   54 (9) 6   81 (   ) 9   5 9 11 14 19

39. 49 (41) 33   61 (67) 73   38 (   ) 20   26 27 28 29 30

40. 85 (94) 9   71 (83) 12   64 (   ) 7   69 70 71 72 73

13. Opposite Meanings

Example: (bright, hot, red)   (colour, cold, burning)

Select two words, one from each bracket, which are opposite in meaning to each other.

Answer: hot and cold.

1. (identical, identity, regular)   (congruent, similar, different)

2. (clear, dull, murky)   (obvious, obtuse, angular)

3. (radiant, radius, revolve)   (rotate, glisten, dull)

4. (straight, lumpy, crumpled)   (upright, crooked, wrinkled)

5. (contaminated, cautious, studious)   (serene, serious, sterile)

6. (sleepy, craggy, alert)   (smooth, uneven, slender)

7. (random, religious, realistic)   (specific, limited, sparse)

8. (explosive, placid, pretend)   (calm, fragile, volatile)

9. (deceitful, hardy, honest)   (devious, delicious, strong)

10. (puncture, punctual, overdue)   (timetable, late, early)

11. (duplex, complete, complex)   (eager, easy, finished)

12. (grotesque, magnificent, mighty)   (powerful, beautiful, ugly)

13. (futile, flimsy, false)   (collapse, weak, rigid)

14. (aggressive, moody, cautious)   (repress, reckless, impatient)

15. (icy, sober, angry)   (cross, solemn, steaming)

16. (stationary, stationery, envelope)   (still, moving, letter)

17. (still, raucous, silent)   (quiet, still, quite)

18. (idol, idle, busy)   (industrious, icon, saintly)

19. (wealthy, poor, humble)   (deliberate, destitute, destroy)

20. (striking, lavish, menial)   (extravagant, opulent, basic)

21. (decorative, bland, simple)   (detailed, unadorned, plush)

22. (fortunate, gracious, grand)   (gifted, unlucky, skilled)

23. (agree, disagree, tolerate)   (oppose, function, flawless)

24. (confession, concise, confusion)   (clarity, mayhem, chaos)

25. (bright, dim, shadowy)   (talented, dingy, reveal)

26. (selfish, selfless, thoughtful)   (arrogant, considerate, miserly)

27. (beauty, harmony, graceful)   (melodic, discord, tuneful)

28. (lead, leash, strap)   (chase, follow, head)

29. (vat, vast, vapour)   (colossal, immense, tiny)

30. (angry, sedate, sparing)   (modest, accurate, serene)

31. (lofty, spacious, confined)   (broad, tall, short)

32. (mobile, rigid, flexible)   (pliable, pleasant, strong)

33. (formal, relaxed, ordered)   (stressed, calm, sedate)

34. (turbulent, tropical, balmy)   (luxurious, choppy, calm)

35. (wild, stormy, jungle)   (animal, fierce, domesticated)

36. (animated, agony, anxiety)   (painless, painful, distressing)

37. (right, answer, solution)   (ignore, respond, correct)

38. (abundant, plentiful, freedom)   (liberate, captivity, liberty)

39. (book, fact, story)   (fiction, reference, library)

40. (focus, device, create)   (disturb, destroy, make)

14. Closest Meanings

Example: (hostile, pleasant, solemn)   (terrible, shy, unfriendly)

Select two words, one from each bracket, which are closest in meaning to each other.

Answer: hostile and unfriendly

.

1. (diverse, same, defeat)   (dainty, different, harsh)

2. (mischievous, graceful, minute)   (clumsy, odour, impish)

3. (tired, artful, anxious)   (painting, calm, sly)

4. (game, set, match)   (harden, soften, melt)

5. (dismiss, encourage, naughty)   (appear, expel, occur)

6. (start, continue, terminate)   (conclude, journey, trek)

7. (fragrant, fragile, frank)   (deceitful, irate, brittle)

8. (minute, hour, decade)   (pretend, petite, annual)

9. (magical, meticulous, mire)   (precise, calamity, slack)

10. (false, fretful, lie)   (answer, anxious, peaceful)

11. (roam, weary, wander)   (elegant, worried, exhausted)

12. (droopy, drowsy, agile)   (sleepy, alert, obtuse)

13. (figure, number, solo)   (single, double, treble)

14. (echo, reply, respond)   (create, cave, repeat)

15. (stench, sturdy, sporadic)   (robust, robot, often)

16. (sprinkled, arid, drenched)   (saturated, moist, dappled)

17. (tasty, tender, tough)   (sweet, sour, flavoursome)

18. (doctor, teacher, pharmacist)   (school, medicine, tutor)

19. (advise, advertise, approach)   (uniform, reform, inform)

20. (dreary, dishevelled, dingy)   (unkempt, uneven, unfair)

21. (ritual, wrath, warrior)   (fury, bravery, army)

22. (tiresome, mundane, serene)   (exciting, tranquil, fearsome)

23. (creative, colourful, dazzling)   (invitation, invention, inventive)

24. (stale, fresh, rancid)   (murky, musty, gloomy)

25. (acrid, arid, acidic)   (parched, sharp, craggy)

26. (lively, livid, vivid)   (sparse, sluggish, furious)

27. (evasive, morose, overjoyed)   (elated, angry, cunning)

28. (dire, pleasant, perfection)   (ample, terrible, frugal)

29. (petrified, secretive, dejected)   (honest, miserable, stressful)

30. (fearsome, feeble, fantastic)   (terrifying, gushing, static)

31. (dashing, daunting, focused)   (formidable, flashy, alert)

32. (accomplished, hopeless, trivial)   (serial, skilful, artistic)

33. (mute, masterful, talkative)   (flattery, chatty, noisy)

34. (energetic, lazy, stagnant)   (active, passive, loathsome)

35. (erase, pause, record)   (data, security, delete)

36. (rigid, correct, formal)   (relaxed, achieve, amend)

37. (hungry, eager, keen)   (fatigue, famished, finished)

38. (debate, refuse, relate)   (discuss, concede, retaliate)

39. (pardon, rot, adore)   (decay, depress, deplore)

40. (confirm, confer, concern)   (value, verify, vindicate)

15. Compound Words

Example: (tar, pop, leg)   (pies, man, day)

Select a word from each bracket which, when put together, create a compound word.

Answer : poppies   (pop + pies)

1. (star, planet, far)   (dark, light, rod)

2. (cat, cap, hood)   (ton, tin, able)

3. (four, for, fore)   (cast, day, hear)

4. (bread, roll, dough)   (dust, crumb, table)

5. (moon, care, sun)   (set, full, tend)

6. (pat, pit, pot)   (chin, ion, try)

7. (miss, mess, once)   (age, old, time)

8. (on, so, too)   (lip, dry, lid)

9. (worst, grand, best)   (play, end, stand)

10. (birth, last, one)   (find, night, day)

11. (for, top, be)   (mend, art, give)

12. (on, an, in)   (art, the, other)

13. (in, good, some)   (den, lid, deed)

14. (book, paper, card)   (bored, board, bred)

15. (on, wit, ant)   (his, them, her)

16. (part, bit, whole)   (sum, cake, some)

17. (fast, wheel, flat)   (car, tyre, barrow)

18. (grew, draw, sketch)   (bridge, some, sum)

19. (coo, ask, walk)   (ten, king, more)

20. (imp, ripe, reap)   (pore, pear, plan)

21. (do, in, out)   (man, ore, main)

22. (cat, trick, don)   (able, key, made)

23. (rat, men, ,low)   (did, age, ion)

24. (fly the, dot)   (red, me, one)

25. (know, no, none)   (left, but, ledge)

26. (tar, flow, sit)   (road, get, down)

27. (on, so, do)   (in, or, at)

28. (to, at, in)   (pin, tack, stick)

29. (ear, nose, foot)   (watch, blood, ring)

30. (eye, tooth, fairy)   (saw, sore, throat)

31. (some, rest, penny)   (more, even, less)

32. (over, turn, flip)   (board, ship, coin)

33. (dish, mop, dust)   (her, mat, cloth)

34. (four, for, fore)   (times, pace, ward)

35. (rest, bed, nap)   (let, ore, ache)

36. (no, not, in)   (here, vice, score)

37. (in, head, four)   (half, fraction, quarters)

38. (over, out, on)   (make, mind, law)

39. (for, be, see)   (me, lock, am)

40. (butter, fresh, full)   (breed, fly, name)

16. Number Letter Codes

Example:

BORE　　**BEND**　　**DENT**　　**CORN**

　　6135　　　8741　　　8136

What does 4781 mean?

What does 6774 mean?

What is the code for TEND?

Using the codes above we know B = 8 as two words start with 8 and two words start with B.

E = 1 as 1 is in both 8741 and 8136. E is the 2nd letter in BEND and the last in BORE

If 81 = BE then 8136 must be BEND

BORE = 8741.

We now know 6135 = DENT as D = 6　E = 1　N = 3 so T = 5

So B = 8　E = 1　N = 3　D = 6　O = 7　R = 4　T = 5

Answer: 4781 = ROBE

**　　　　6774 = DOOR**

**　　　　TEND = 5136**

1. **FULL**　　**FLAP**　　**LEAP**　　**LEAF**
　　　2146　　**5322**　　**5246**

a) What is the code for PALE?

　6142　　6421　　2146　　6412　　2156

b) What does 5112 mean?

　FLEA　FULL　LEAF　FEEL　FLUE

c) What does 6142 mean?

　PLEA　PULL　PEAL　FLEE　PULP

2. **BARE**　　　**CRAB**　　**CARE**　　　**RATE**
　　　1263　　　**4213**　　**5124**

a) What is the code for RACE?

　1321　　1253　　5124　　4213　　1235

b) What does 4321 mean?

　BARE　　BEAR　　BEER　　CRIB　　CRAB

c) What does 1321 mean?

　BEAT　　BOAT　　RACE　　REAR　　READ

3. SAME   MAST   MESS   TEST
    4211   4315   1342

a) What is the code for TEST?

   5215   5234   5231   4315   4211

b) What is the code for MEAT?

   4315   1224   4235   1234   4311

c) What does 5342 mean?

   TEAM   TAME   TEAS   MAST   TEST

4. POUR   INTO   NOTE   TOUR
    8456   4657   1623

a) What is the code for ROPE?

   3284   3617   3665   2485   4764

b) What does 1845 mean?

   PINE   PINT   POUR   TURN   REIN

c) What does 5234 mean?

   TOUR   TUNE   TURN   NONE   NINE

5. DRAB   BALD   BLOW   WARD
**   4235   4621   1764**

a) What is the code for WARD?

   5671   5331   5361   4615   4372

b) What is the code for LOAD?

   6251   2761   2561   2361   6351

c) What does 7361 mean?

   ROAD   RODE   RAIL   LOAD   LEAD

6. TRIP   INTO   TINT   PAIN
**   5621   3725   2134**

a) What is the code for PINT?

   5673   5213   5613   2134   5447

b) What does 7621 mean?

   PAIN   NOTE   RAIN   RATE   ROAR

c) What does 5473 mean?

   PART   PANT   POOR   PORT   PAIN

7. RICE   EPIC   CARE   PACE
     4153   3264   6534

a) What is the code for PACE?

1234   1264   3214   3261   5346

b) What is the code for RACE?

6534   6421   1426   6234   1256

c) What does 1546 mean?

PIER   PEAR   PAIR   AREA   PACE

8. PRAM   MARE   PEAT   MEAT
     4162   3215   3614

a) What is the code for TAPE?

5142 5216   5132   5613   5165

b) What does 6152 mean?

REAM   RAMP   PART   PERT   RATE

c) What does 5613 mean?

TEAR   TRAP   TEAM   TRIP   TAME

9. **DEER**   **DICE**   **HERB**   **ICED**
　　　5324   7631   1332

a) What is the code for CRIB?

6313　　5713　　5331　　6274　　4721

b) What does 5321 mean?

HEED　　HIRE　　HERD　　HERB　　HERE

c) What does 4721 mean?

DIRE　　BRED　　BIDE　　BIRD　　DEER

10. **FLOW**   **WAKE**   **BAKE**   **LEAK**
　　　4215   3215   8673

a) What is the code for LEAK?

6771　　6521　　6728　　3768　　3215

b) What does 4673 mean?

BLOB　　BOWL　　BEAK　　BLOW　　BLEW

c) What does 3261 mean?

LAKE　　WOLF　　LOOK　　WOKE　　WALK

11. DARK   LAME   CALM   CARE
**   7182   6152   3154**

a) What is the code for CALM?

6332   6178   8352   8142   6152

b) What is the code for RACE?

5213   5142   5162   7213   7162

c) What does 3217 mean?

DELL   DALE   DEAD   DARE   DEAL

12. POLO   DOLL   FOLD   PLOD
**   4313   4135   2315**

a) What is the code for LOAD?

1325   1365   2134   1362   2315

b) What is the code for DOLL?

2134   4135   5311   2164   1362

c) What does 2361 mean?

FLOW   FOAL   FOOL   LOOP   LOAF

13. **EACH**   **ECHO**   **CAME**   **DOME**
   6754   **3154**   **4132**

a) What is the code for HEAD?

   5764   2754   2776   2416   5784

b) What does 2776 mean?

   HOME   HEAR   HOOD   MOOD   ROAD

c) What does 2754 mean?

   MORE   HERE   HARE   HOME   MARE

14. **FARM**   **RAKE**   **REAM**   **MAKE**
   2165   **4123**   **2513**

a) What is the code for MAKE?

   3126   3165   4123   3125   4165

b) What does 4165 mean?

   FARM   MARE   FAKE   REEK   FEAR

c) What does 3126 mean?

   RAKE   MEEK   RARE   MARK   MARE

17. Making A Middle Word

Example: bond (band) tail

core (   ) sand

Answer: care

Make the word in brackets following the same pattern as above.

```
1  34      2
b o n d ( band ) t a i l
```

```
1  34        2
c o r e ( c a r e ) s a n d
```

If there is a choice where the letter has been taken from write all the options down and select the one which makes a proper word.

```
      13  2          4
Example:  s a v e ( s e a m )  m a d e
```

```
      13 2          4              1              4 32
      f e a t  (          ) d a l e    OR    f e a t(          ) d a l e
```

Answer: f e e d

	Multiple Choice Answers
1. dare (time) mint nine ( ) same	earn ease easy vase care
2. mind (inch) each dove ( ) veer	oven open over ache oval
3. draw (wink) kind port ( ) doll	told tail toil prod drop

4. lever (earn) lean
    opens (   ) gnat

    nape pant neat past pane

5. black (kerb) earn
    mill   (   ) oboe

    lobe loom lime mile bell

6. storm (vest) every
    sorry (   ) talon

    slat atom also alas tool

7. blend (blew) crew
    shame (   ) crow

    crew come shot sham show

8. frog (germ) meet
    four (   ) tour

    rout root turf roof fret

9. extra (fox) sofa
    atom (   ) dart

    mat ram rot rat mad

10. cream (room) motor
    odour (   ) seven

    need deer rude dove dens

11. photo (hate) same
    after (   ) blow

    flow flew fore fret flaw

12. space (cap) price
    dodge (   ) dream

    arm age add gem ego

13. flake (done) pond
    river (   ) pout

    tier trip trot veto tour

14. cliff   (fish) horse
    drawn (   ) eleven

    nave wean near wave ware

15. pour (rope) pole
    dash (   ) need

    head hash hand heed send

16. brave (vest) store
    scone (   ) storm   neat near nest news nose

17. trial (stay) pushy
    niece (   ) whole   coin once coil hole nice

18. crime (fire) force
    knows (   ) brand   boss bond bran brow band

19. stand (date) mauve
    cliff (   ) forum   form fill foil film fool

20. branch (hard) board
    mature (   ) chars   each ache stem eats ears

21. stale (vale) leave
    cream (   ) piety   type time team tear tram

22. reach (chin) vein
    feast (   ) crop   step stop pore pest fore

23. graph (hope) roped
    teams (   ) fares   same safe seem seam seat

24. panel (peal) layer
    tripe (   ) clear   tire tape tear tore tale

25. label (call) scrap
    bodge (   ) pride   rode robe rope ride reed

26. laugh (ugly) yacht
    filed (   ) tribe   lift left lied leer loft

27. train (trap) price
    newel (   ) terse   rest nest newt went sent

28. flare (beam) crumb
    tense (   ) ghost

        test tens tent tone tons

29. sleep (pace) reach
    blend (   ) wrong

        drew doll door done grow

30. crime (maid) dream
    crest (   ) poles

        sets stop seep slop spot

31. force (your) hurry
    sandy (   ) fresh

        hand hens here hare hear

32. while (halt) stand
    about (   ) felon

        bolt belt blue blob blub

33. pill   (limp) mile
    ease (   ) mare

        seam ream rear seem same

34. harsh (hand) dance
    bored (   ) dull

        bull bore bold bled bred

35. gentle (real) charms
    straps (   ) floats

        toss past atop arts asps

36. trust (step) depth
    close (   ) bathe

        scab seat seal bath base

37. chase (hate) hotel
    bloom (   ) hover

        home lore loom hole love

38. trail   (liar) grace
    cloud (   ) leper

        door done dupe dull dour

39. panel (swan) wings
    cream (   ) anger

        rang rare rage race ream

40. black (kerb) brave
    horse (   ) timid   sore time emit stir edit

18. Coding And Decoding Words

A B C D E F G H I J K L M N O P Q R S T U V W X Y Z

Example: If the code for TAKE is UBJD what is the code for PRAM?

The word has been put into code by moving forward 1 letter for the first 2 letters then backwards 1 for the last 2 letters
T forward 1 is U
A forward 1 is B
K backwards 1 is J
E backwards 1 is D

Copy this code to put PRAM into code

Answer: QSZL

Example 2: If the code for TRACE is ROWXY what does DOKRH mean?

T moves back 2 to become R
R moves back 3 to become O
A moves back 4 to become W
C moves back 5 to become X
E moves back 6 to become Y

To decipher the code do the opposite.

D forwards 2 is F
O forwards 3 is R
K forwards 4 is O
R forward 5 is W
H forwards 6 is N

Answer: FROWN

1. If the code for SCALE is VAEMC. What is the code for DANCE?

   GYRDC   GXRBC   FYRDC   FXRBC   GZRAC

2. If the code for RAIL is SCLP. What is the code for EXTRA?

   DYXVF   FZVWE   FZWVF   DVQWE   EZQVF

3. If the code for BOOT is AMLP. What is the code for DAME?

   CYKB   CYJB   CZJA   CYJA   DXKA

4. If the code for PIANO is RGCLQ. What is the code for WRONG?

   YPQPI   YQMKI   YPMPH   XPQKH   YPQLI

5. If the code for BLAME is FIEJI. What is the code for MICE?

   QFHB   QFGB   QFFB   PFHC   PGFC

6. If the code for ANGRY is CPITA. What is the code for FRAME?

   GTCDF   HTCOG   HTCPG   HSCOG   GSCPF

7. If the code for MONEY is PMQCB. What is the code for PEACE?

   SCDAH   SCDAI   SBDAH   SCDBH   RBDAI

8. If the code for HARSH is GDQVG. What is the code for EMPTY?

   DPOXY   CPOXY   DPOWX   DQNWX   DPNWX

9. If the code for PHONE is QJRRJ. What is the code for HORSE?

   IQUXJ   IQUXK   JQUWJ   IQUWJ   IRUXK

10. If the code for MUSIC is KRODW. What is the code for CLAP?

AJWK　　AIWK　　ZIWJ　　AIVK　　BIVJ

11. If the code for RADIO is SCGMO. What does PRHR mean?

OPAL　　OPEN　　OXEN　　QUIZ　　QUAD

12. If the code for COACH is FQDEK. What does GKUV mean?

DIVE　　JINX　　DIRT　　JOKE　　DOGS

13. If the code for MEAT is LCXP. What does EJFL mean?

DOVE　　FLOP　　DIET　　FLIP　　FLEX

14. If the code for CRIME is EPKKG. What does IPQUP mean?

GROWN　　KINGS　　GROWL　　KEEPS　　GROAN

15. If the code for RICH is QHBG. What does GDKO mean?

HEAP　　HELP　　HEAL　　FEEL　　FELT

16. If the code for APPLE is CTVTO. What does NSBM mean?

POND　　LONE　　POLE　　LOVE　　LOCH

17. If the code for FACE is GBEG. What does NPNG mean?

MOLE　　MORE　　ONCE　　MILE　　OVER

18. If the code for PLANK is SKDMN. What does EQLMJ mean?

BRIDE　　CRUMB　　BRING　　HORSE　　BRIBE

19. If the code for HUNTS is GVMUR. What does LBMHN mean?

MATCH   MANTA   NOBLE   MANGO   NAMES

20. If the code for FENCE is JIRGI. What does XMKIV mean?

BINGO   TIGER   TILER   TIARA   BUILD

21. If the code for FORCE is HMTAG. What is the code for BLIND?

DJQLF   DJKQF   CKLMF   DJKLF   ZJMLF

22. If the code for DRESS is ETHWX. What is the code for GLOVE?

HNRRJ   HNRZJ   HNSRJ   FNRZJ   FMRZJ

23. If the code for BELL is CDMK. What is the code for ROSE?

SNTD   SNTF   SNRD   SPTD   SNRF

24. If the code for PONY is OMKU. What is the code for HILT?

GOP   GGIP   GGOP   GKIQ   FGIP

25. If the code for REACH is VCEAL. What is the code for BELT?

FCQS   GCPR   FCPR   FCPS   XCPR

26. If the code for IRON is FOLK. What is the code for YOLK?

BLIH   VLIH   VLJH   VLHI   BLJH

27. If the code for BEST is XIOX. What is the code for HAND?

DEJH   CEJI   DEIH   CFJH   DFIH

28. If the code for HELP is IGOT. What is the code for ABLE?

BDRI   BCOI   BDPI   BCPI   BDOI

29. If the code for RACE is LVYB. What is the code for WALK?

QVGH   QVIH   QVHH   QTGH   RTHH

30. If the code for SPOIL is WMSFP. What is the code for PURSE?

TRVOI   TRVPI   TRVVI   TSVPI   TSVOI

31. If the code for FRUIT is GQVHU. What does TBFMF mean?

SCONE   SCENE   SCARE   UNDER   SCORE

32. If the code for HARSH is KDUVK. What does WUXWK mean?

TRACE   TRIBE   TRUTH   TRACK   TRAIL

33. If the code for FINAL is DMLEJ. What does HIJPW mean?

JEWEL   JERKY   FIEND   JELLY   FEARS

34. If the code for TRAIL is QTXKI. What does TCQEE mean?

WITCH   WATCH   WHICH   WAITS   WATER

35. If the code for CRAFT is BSZGS. What does FMZTR mean?

GLASS   GLOWS   GLOSS   ENJOY   ENTER

36. If the code for WRITE is TVFXB. What does CPRXB mean?

FLAME   FLOOR   ZEBRA   FLARE   FLUTE

37. If the code for BULL is YFOO. What does YZPV mean?

BIKE   BAKE   BARE   BONE   BANE

38. If the code for BEEF is YVVU. What does RXVW mean?

ICON   SCAN   ICED   IDLE   SKID

39. If the code for GAME is TZNV. What does DRXP mean?

WALK   WICK   WIND   WIRE   WAND

40. If the code for HIDE is SRWV. What does OZPV mean?

LOVE   LIKE   LANE   LAKE   LACE

ANSWERS

Section 1 – Letter Sequences

1.	NP	21.	YD
2.	SD	22.	DS
3.	GY	23.	XP
4.	SK	24.	GB
5.	JQ	25.	NQ
6.	XS	26.	MI
7.	GT	27.	CT
8.	LU	28.	CX
9.	TS	29.	ZC
10.	QW	30.	NH
11.	JU	31.	RB
12.	IR	32.	UJ
13.	RM	33.	EP
14.	KV	34.	TE
15.	HJ	35.	GI
16.	VH	36.	HW
17.	TF	37.	FR
18.	BS	38.	CT
19.	AQ	39.	DM
20.	OJ	40.	LM

Section 2 – Letter Pairs

1.	LW	21.	TP
2.	EV	22.	GS
3.	TF	23.	GG
4.	YL	24.	OR
5.	ZZ	25.	HL
6.	IG	26.	GV
7.	SW	27.	SF
8.	BF	28.	JG
9.	GJ	29.	PS
10.	CJ	30.	YH
11.	US	31.	QS
12.	HT	32.	SD
13.	DW	33.	EQ
14.	AZ	34.	GR
15.	VI	35.	XG
16.	QL	36.	SD
17.	OT	37.	FK
18.	EB	38.	BS
19.	WC	39.	LP
20.	PC	40.	RV

Section 3 – Three Letter Words   Section 4 – Odd Words Out

1.	ore	21.	hop
2.	ten	22.	ear
3.	pen	23.	lea
4.	can	24.	pet
5.	low	25.	rag
6.	amp	26.	red
7.	ten	27.	and
8.	ion	28.	ate
9.	cat	29.	ash
10.	low	30.	den
11.	eat	31.	rib
12.	ace	32.	hoe
13.	ice	33.	man
14.	wit	34.	the
15.	ire	35.	eel
16.	ran	36.	pen
17.	con	37.	lad
18.	ask	38.	arc
19.	row	39.	ink
20.	hat	40.	man

1.	sun/hot	21.	sky/air
2.	grin/discover	22.	table/phone
3.	fly/swim	23.	latch/point
4.	relay/hurdle	24.	jester/lady
5.	football/rugby	25.	raven/battle
6.	gold/silver	26.	finger/card
7.	liver/foot	27.	letter/sentence
8.	lace/plastic	28.	tiny/third
9.	pint/gallon	29.	day/tomorrow
10.	apple/pear	30.	daisy/school
11.	denim/cotton	31.	dodge/gulp
12.	field/paddock	32.	wise/cut
13.	view/cold	33.	word/bang
14.	paint/add	34.	record/radio
15.	book/music	35.	support/start
16.	cup/fork	36.	red/onion
17.	hamper/hinder	37.	sky/sea
18.	spade/plate	38.	worm/snail
19.	cap/shoe	39.	piano/cheese
20.	call/look	40.	ewe/mare

Section 5 – Move One Letter

1. T	21. P
2. O	22. D
3. I	23. O
4. E	24. R
5. I	25. P
6. R	26. R
7. C	27. N
8. P	28. S
9. C	29. T
10. T	30. D
11. H	31. R
12. E	32. R
13. U	33. H
14. I	34. R
15. L	35. G
16. S	36. C
17. U	37. C
18. C	38. L
19. N	39. S
20. N	40. H

Section 6 – Start/End Letters

1. D	21. E
2. H	22. P
3. W	23. W
4. Y	24. W
5. A	25. T
6. E	26. T
7. B	27. E
8. F	28. R
9. G	29. B
10. L	30. H
11. M	31. K
12. B	32. Y
13. R	33. O
14. S	34. L
15. H	35. A
16. H	36. N
17. G	37. D
18. G	38. M
19. K	39. P
20. N	40. R

Section 7 – Two Meanings

1. firm	21. fair
2. sweet	22. cane
3. craft	23. trifle
4. fire	24. snake
5. plague	25. pepper
6. tackle	26. shift
7. snap	27. squash
8. chair	28. trip
9. log	29. figure
10. cross	30. puzzle
11. shine	31. iron
12. harbour	32. bowl
13. storm	33. reflect
14. haul	34. belt
15. coat	35. mirror
16. shower	36. comb
17. foil	37. shade
18. felt	38. dog
19. train	39. wrench
20. stem	40. pass

Section 8 – Hidden 4 Letter Words

1. chin	21. gnat
2. thin	22. fear
3. chop	23. area
4. were	24. army
5. them	25. rail
6. meat	26. vein
7. tram	27. seem
8. edge	28. open
9. idea	29. tool
10. sour	30. oven
11. scar	31. oxen
12. seat	32. them
13. tyre	33. belt
14. taxi	34. herb
15. ache	35. hero
16. sink	36. pear
17. hiss	37. your
18. hate	38. ball
19. lean	39. soil
20. seat	40. term

Section 9 – Algebra

1i.	16	5i.	C
ii.	9	ii.	A
iii.	38	iii.	D
iv.	19	iv.	E
v.	100	v.	B
2 i.	92	6i.	C
ii.	0	ii.	D
iii.	44	iii.	E
iv.	2	iv.	C
v.	64	v.	A
3 i.	40	7i.	E
ii.	60	ii.	A
iii.	39	iii.	D
iv.	25	iv.	D
v.	105	v.	C
4i.	30	8 i.	C
ii.	103	ii.	E
iii.	40	iii.	A
iv.	29	iv.	C
v.	19	v.	D

Section 10 – Complete Number sentence

1.	9	21.	5
2.	2	22.	4
3.	4	23.	8
4.	4	24.	10
5.	60	25.	13
6.	7	26.	30
7.	30	27.	11
8.	1	28.	7
9.	20	29.	10
10.	3	30.	12
11.	3	31.	20
12.	4	32.	12
13.	7	33.	26
14.	5	34.	40
15.	5	35.	2
16.	4	36.	12
17.	9	37.	5
18.	7	38.	4
19.	2	39.	8
20.	12	40.	25

Section 11 – Number sequences

1.	15	21.	12.5
2.	64	22.	63
3.	18	23.	9
4.	39	24.	71
5.	120	25.	100
6.	45	26.	44
7.	80	27.	12
8.	44	28.	32
9.	61	29.	30
10.	240	30.	5
11.	75	31.	21
12.	24	32.	360
13.	71	33.	25
14.	83	34.	120
15.	73	35.	32
16.	88	36.	37
17.	26	37.	36
18.	3	38.	29
19.	57	39.	69
20.	3	40.	45

Section 12 – Missing number in bracket

1.	20	21.	120
2.	41	22.	34
3.	36	23.	20
4.	25	24.	74
5.	12	25.	44
6.	40	26.	55
7.	28	27.	18
8.	25	28.	32
9.	37	29.	21
10.	8	30.	19
11.	10	31.	89
12.	41	32.	27
13.	24	33.	6
14.	3	34.	20
15.	52	35.	59
16.	31	36.	72
17.	60	37.	37
18.	12	38.	9
19.	60	39.	29
20.	45	40.	71

Section 13 – Opposite Meanings

1. identical & different
2. clear & obtuse
3. radiant & dull
4. straight & crooked
5. contaminated & sterile
6. craggy & smooth
7. random & specific
8. placid & volatile
9. honest & devious
10. punctual & late
11. complex & easy
12. grotesque & beautiful
13. flimsy & rigid
14. cautious & reckless
15. icy & steaming
16. stationary & moving
17. raucous & quiet
18. idle & industrious
19. wealthy & destitute
20. lavish & basic
21. decorative & unadorned
22. fortunate & unlucky
23. agree & oppose
24. confusion & clarity
25. bright & dingy
26. selfish & considerate
27. harmony & discord
28. lead & follow
29. vast & tiny
30. angry & serene
31. lofty & short
32. rigid & pliable
33. relaxed & stressed
34. turbulent & calm
35. wild & domesticated
36. agony & painless
37. answer & ignore
38. freedom & captivity
39. fact & fiction
40. create & destroy

Section 14 – Closest Meanings

1. diverse & different
2. mischievous & impish
3. artful & sly
4. set & harden
5. dismiss & expel
6. terminate & conclude
7. fragile & brittle
8. minute & petite
9. meticulous & precise
10. fretful & anxious
11. weary & exhausted
12. drowsy & sleepy
13. solo & single
14. echo & repeat
15. sturdy & robust
16. drenched & saturated
17. tasty & flavoursome
18. teacher & tutor
19. advise & inform
20. dishevelled & unkempt
21. wrath & fury
22. serene & tranquil
23. creative & inventive
24. stale & musty
25. arid & parched
26. livid & furious
27. overjoyed & elated
28. dire & terrible
29. dejected & miserable
30. fearsome & terrifying
31. daunting & formidable
32. accomplished & skilful
33. talkative & chatty
34. energetic & active
35. erase & delete
36. correct & amend
37. hungry & famished
38. debate & discuss
39. rot & decay
40. confirm & verify

Section 15 - Compound Words

1. starlight
2. capable
3. forecast
4. breadcrumb
5. sunset
6. potion
7. message
8. solid
9. grandstand
10. birthday
11. forgive
12. another
13. indeed
14. cardboard
15. wither
16. wholesome
17. wheelbarrow
18. drawbridge
19. cooking
20. reappear
21. domain
22. donkey
23. ration
24. theme
25. knowledge
26. target
27. door
28. attack
29. earring
30. eyesore
31. restless
32. overboard
33. dishcloth
34. forward
35. restore
36. novice
37. headquarters
38. outlaw
39. beam
40. butterfly

Section 16- Number/Letter Codes

1a) 6421
 b) feel
 c) peal
2a) 1253
 b) bear
 c) rear
3a) 5215
 b) 4235
 c) tame
4a) 3617
 b) pint
 c) turn
5a) 5671
 b) 2361
 c) road
6a) 5213
 b) rain
 c) port
7a) 1234
 b) 6234
 c) pier

8a) 5132
 b) rate
 c) trap
9a) 6274
 b) herd
 c) bird
10a) 6521
 b) blow
 c) walk
11a) 6178
 b) 5162
 c) deal
12a) 1365
 b) 5311
 c) foal
13a) 2416
 b) hood
 c) home
14a) 3165
 b) fake
 c) mark

Section 17 – Making the Middle Word

1. ease
2. over
3. told
4. past
5. loom
6. also
7. show
8. root
9. rat
10. deer
11. flew
12. add
13. tour
14. wave
15. hand
16. nest
17. once
18. bond
19. film
20. ears
21. team
22. stop
23. same
24. tale
25. robe
26. left
27. newt
28. tens
29. done
30. seep
31. hare
32. blue
33. same
34. bold
35. atop
36. seat
37. love
38. dupe
39. rare
40. edit

Section 18 – Coding/Decoding

1. GYRDC
2. FZWVF
3. CYJA
4. YPQLI
5. QFGB
6. HTCOG
7. SCDAH
8. DPOWX
9. IQUWJ
10. AIWK
11. OPEN
12. DIRT
13. FLIP
14. GROWN
15. HELP
16. LOVE
17. MOLE
18. BRING
19. MANGO
20. TIGER
21. DJKLF
22. HNRZJ
23. SNTD
24. GGIP
25. FCPR
26. VLIH
27. DEJH
28. BDOI
29. QVHH
30. TRVPI
31. SCENE
32. TRUTH
33. JELLY
34. WATCH
35. GLASS
36. FLUTE
37. BAKE
38. ICED
39. WICK
40. LAKE

—

Printed in Poland
by Amazon Fulfillment
Poland Sp. z o.o., Wrocław

54929455R00045